This book is given to:

_____

╔═══════════════════════╗
T O D A Y ~
╚═══════════════════════╝

On this _____ *day of* _____

In the year of _____

From: _____

Occasion: _____

Today

Written and Illustrated by:

Vivian L Childs

CEO: Minister Vivian L. Childs
CFO: Dr. Henry Childs
COO: Rev. Henry Childs II, J.D.
Director of Operations: Dr. Ashante Y. Everett
Director of Marketing: Nakeisha M. Curry, M.D.

V.L. Childs/U.I.C.F LLC
P.O. Box 9334
Warner Robins, GA 31095
vlccreations@yahoo.com

First published by V.L. Childs 4/21/2009
ISBN 978-0-9799896-2-9

Author and Illustrator: Vivian L. Childs
Editors: Mack Curry III, Nakeisha M. Curry, Ashante Y. Everett
Layout design: Vivian L. Childs

About the Author~

Vivian L. Childs is a minister and the daughter of Helen and the late Senior Chief Isaiah Clark of Atlanta, Georgia. She is married to Rev-Colonel Dr. Henry Childs, USAF retired, who is the pastor of North Bethlehem Missionary Baptist church where Vivian is a minister and the First Lady. Together, they are blessed with remarkable children and grandchildren.

Vivian has served in many capacities and has been recognized for many outstanding achievements Her love for writing began at an early age, but culminated when she became the Elementary/Middle School Principal of a Christian school, coupled with her many travels that blessed her to appreciate God's glorious wonders of living in diverse cultures.

I pray you will enjoy the artwork in this book. I was blessed to take a painting class from a renown artist, and I wanted to share it with you, the reader. I was fascinated with what could be accomplished with a brush and some paint. The painting on the next page has been manipulated in many ways, on the following pages, to share my thoughts.

Thank you Diana C. for an awesome night shared among friends. Be blessed~

Today
is the
beginning
of tomorrow

and
the end
of
yesterday.

Today
touches the
soul

and

wipes

the

tears

away.

Today

frees

the mind

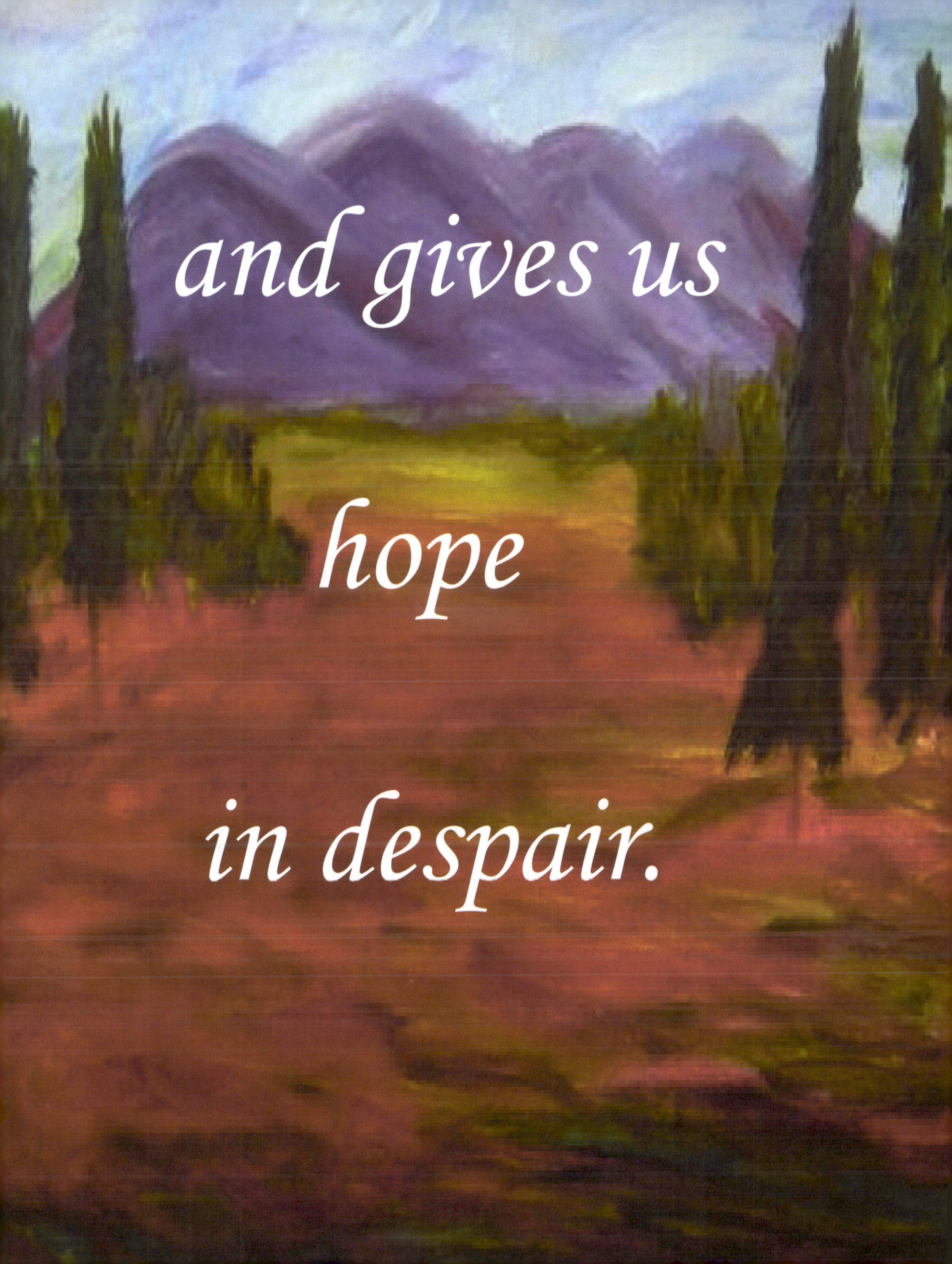

and gives us

hope

in despair.

Today

comforts

the

body

in the sway of a

rocking chair..

Today brings out

the sunshine in

the twinkling of

an eye.

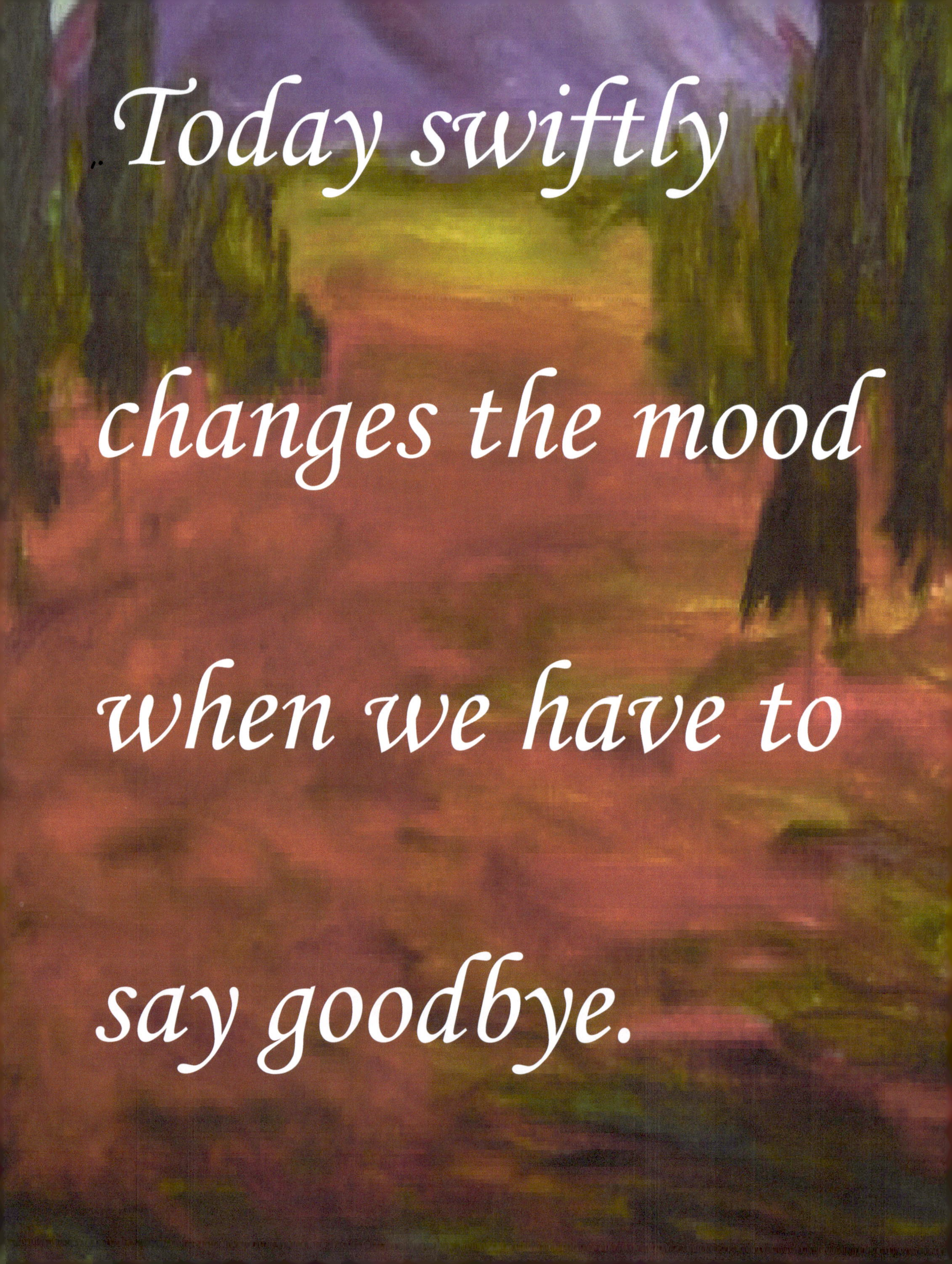
Today swiftly
changes the mood
when we have to
say goodbye.

Goodbye

So, farewell
again
today,

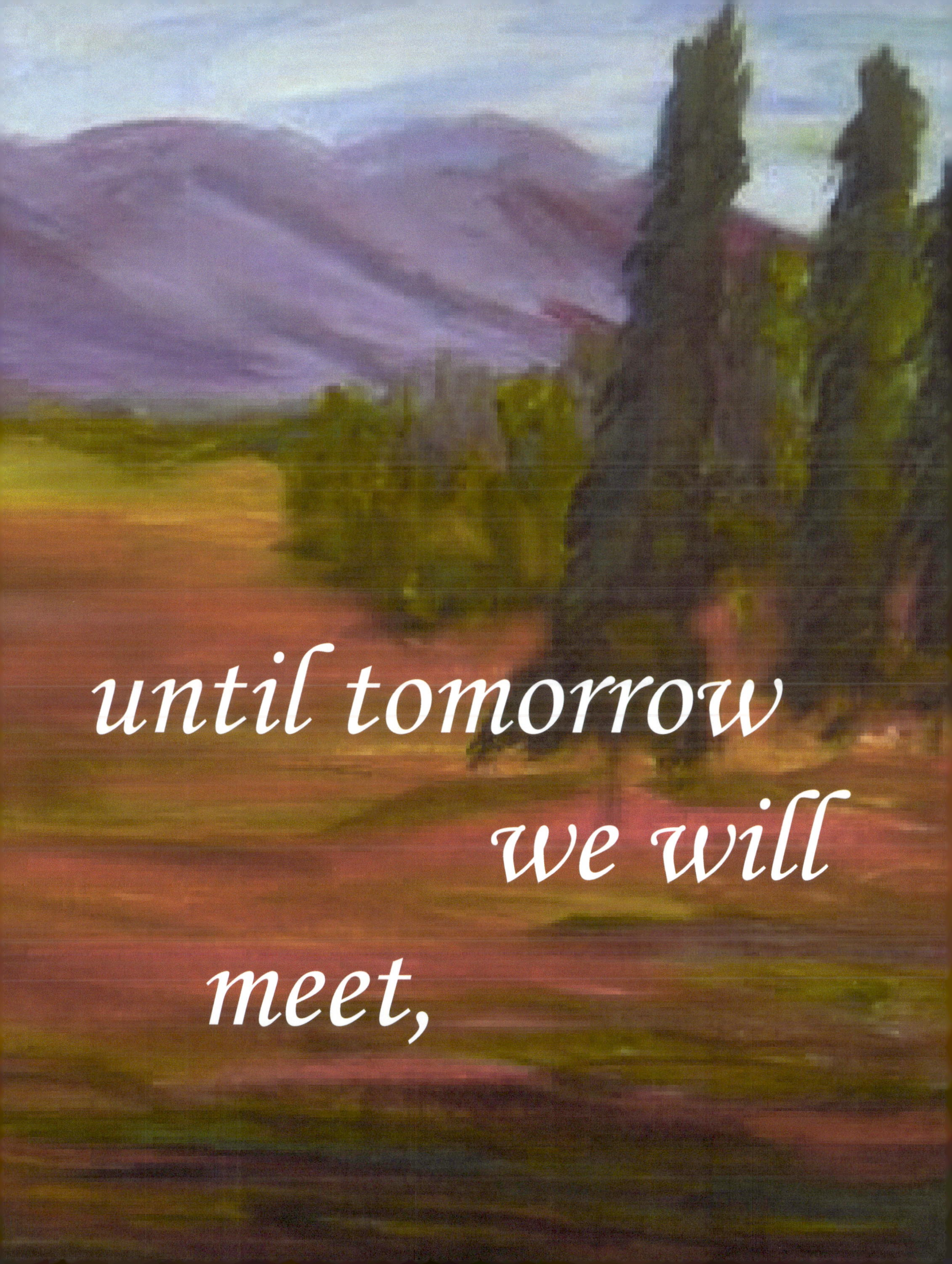
until tomorrow
we will
meet,

and begin this

process again,

after a good

night's sleep.

The End

www.ingramcontent.com/pod-product-compliance
Lightning Source LLC
LaVergne TN
LVHW072123070426
835511LV00002B/80